DEFENSIVE STRATEGIES

ROBERT BENSE

Bob

Belle Fontaine Editions

DEFENSIVE STRATEGIES

Poems

Poems within have been widely published in national poetry magazines. This is a privately published and printed book. (The figures and narratives herein are purely imaginary, including the voice in the first person.)

ISBN-13: 978-0-9965018-3-5
LCCN: 2016954037

Published by Belle Fontaine Editions
509 Hartnell Place
Sacramento, CA 95825

ALSO BY ROBERT BENSE

Poetry

River Road: a Mississippi
Listening to the Bowl Crack
Arguments in a Public Space
Readings in Ordinary Time

for Sonya

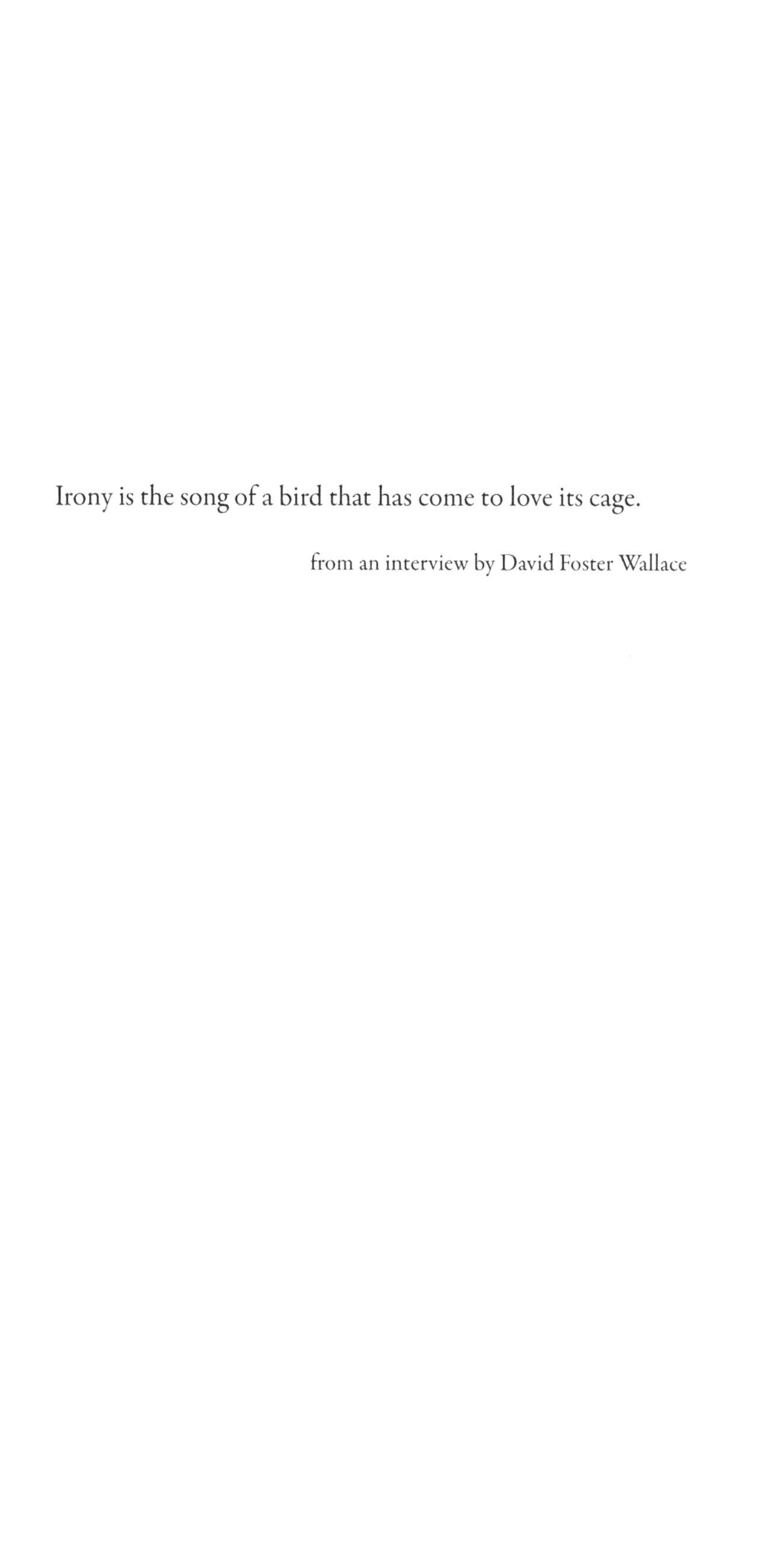

Irony is the song of a bird that has come to love its cage.

from an interview by David Foster Wallace

Contents

One

Two

Three

Four

Five

Six

One

Belles Lettres

Starting with the letters, we learn
the *A* of ah.
Eventually, the *O* of awe.
Along with mistakes of a day.
Errors of a life.
The undistributed, deserted middle.
So happiness is a false conclusion
if you ask around.
But lips of those who should know
are sealed.

Force of Elementary Matters

Once again treason of matter is in the air.
Leaf fall. Quantum theory. Sarcomas. Sly
encryptions of *The Da Vinci Code*. Menace
trailing three Victorian paces.
                                        They know
one another. Stepping out from these narrow
side streets. Those dark addresses of pain.
The slack-jawed shadows.
                                    One leg up
on us, the moon rides easy to a new
gated quarter. Shutting its eye on suffering
and old dead drops of the heart:
                                            the world
a sting operation of shrinking innocence, if ever.
Witnesses inside pulling shades. *Pari passu*.
The material of what matters has lost its youth.

After Baudelaire

First the inquisition. This may take
days. They will ask your name
in different ways. The fat man with
a pad. A thin man in glasses.
They will look for answers
to unasked questions.
And there may be choices like
Do you take sugar?
to lower your guard.
Some things you can be fairly certain
are not to be said. Like names.
Perhaps you would have preferred
being ignored. That is not an option.
When it comes, the pain will exceed
your wishes. Nightmares, the roaches
a searchlight in the eyes
are not likely to be about truth.
Interrogation has just begun.

Travelers

In fact we've packed almost
everything in sight. Cold fright
at the precipice. The long
thought of dying.
                    These bus
windows have cracked glass.
Sun film peels from
a two-way mirror.
                    We notice
what we see notices us.
A mountain, an unmade bed
of tar stare back. But an ostrich
buries its familiar head.
                              At the town
gates no one waits. No one meets
us in the square. The tongue we speak
no one knows.
                    In the hostel
we unpack what we thought we forgot.
Roll of the dice. And aftermath to last
since all the shops close at six.

Guarding Paradise: a theodicy

Sidewalk tenements of cardboard.
Trickle of urine and a pigeon.
Shadowy men with holy grievances
stopping traffic.

Broken glass of villa walls
guarding putative gardens of bliss.
Your hands still bleeding.

Messages between the Cyclopses
and the Underworld hacked.

Three men hosing the pavement.
They're guarding paradise.
That's your blood on the concrete.

Razor wire slicing the sun.
All afternoon winds of constant sorrow
at thirty knots. Searchlights scanning
low for your flight from anxious night.

Cracked lenses of the stars.
Abyss of furtive darknesses
dithery like shortwave.

You will be cleared through at the frontier
but only if you have suffered enough.

Reflection in the Rearview

Renunciation fits the mind
as a necessary exercise

for finding purpose
after some excess

the overturned chairs at loud tables
all those days passed in exaggeration

and after too many silly chardonnays
your Patagonian tour endlessly spun

quiet at self's aggrandizing center
calms the universe

days on end now, a single canoe
on the glass of a languid river

the worn hills calling out
for falling leaves and shadows

one slows down, in case the purpose
of almost everything

like grisaille and ice
is easy to miss.

A Question of Geography

Those coast lines on thick paper
have coarsened
like an old coastal range
to keep us from falling off.
Swedenborg believed geography
is not about maps.
Roads seldom take the shortest
way to where you're going.
And elevations of the interior
are never high enough
for the long perspective.
France, a case in point. Think of
Bordeaux at the edge of a large bay
and Montaigne in his Spanish
angularity. Writing with the equanimity
of broad views against the narrow.
Or Bernadette in the darkness of her
grotto administering correctives
to Persephone at the wide margins
where miracle and swindle co-exist.
With all the others, coats on, you wait
looking for somewhere
and unsure how to get there.

Failure of the Maps

We've come from
somewhere
in the dark.
Headed for
who knows.
Pain, angry
mad, is driving.
I'm in the back
trying to hold my tongue.
The body
wants out.
I name streets:
if not this, at the next
light. I try
appeals.
Drop names. Some
you've heard.
Next the grey
institutionals.
Baptist. General.
Worry reaches my gut.

Nurses chatter
just out of hearing.
The odd hours, red
lines. Buzz of
small motors.
Detective work.
And when tracked down
won't it give
a false address?

Change as Principle

The change comes like
voluble ice.
Cracking of limbs
up and down winter's reach.
Old tire tracks spun out
of the mountains
leaving no direction.
Because no direction
has been found
space spreads to
accommodate the predictable
like rigged markets
in the inevitable.
Soon the burly forests
awaken to the snore
of saws. From a cabin
I listen to the loud rings
of old trees.
The sun tips through branches.
But only the agile
turn around fast enough
to see the morning's evening
shadows shuffle in.

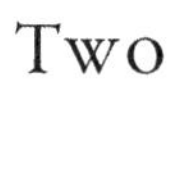

After an Inquiry into Silence

It hangs motionless in air like
the Holy Ghost. Wings
scarcely beating. Yet viscous.
Physical—and high maintenance.
(The hedges aren't likely to have
been clipped.) There are addresses.
Addresses that can change
with a nod. Travel is necessary
and the destination may be
another state. An amplitude
of the second order
like exhaustion or wealth.
Arriving, you'll have to ignore fields
loud with locust sibilances.
The cow bawling many fences over
and two jets spreading contrails.
Then you notice windows without
panes. Doors opened to wind.
Absence sharing its features
with the vanished.
The past as it is
and never silence as it was.

Solving for the Unknown

They're off to the Outer Banks
for fun. They're buying
propane and sunscreen
for their rental. But they're
headed to rooms with tight
thin walls. And narrow halls.
Low clouds that sweep in
with a storm. Water dragging
its wet blanket across the beach.
They will practice
solitary offertories
on desultory afternoons.
Dusting furniture. Closing
windows for whoever comes next.
Gift, giving, and giver
will have become indivisible
in a small mathematics.
They will turn the key twice
one last time.

The Sixth Proof of God

Passions pass while you're still looking
for endless spring. A particle's slow
decay. Once I thought I wanted to see
the world in sunglasses. Unlikely
haunts of dust. Sand fringed with palms.
You know the postcards.

But soon the quarter moon rests again
on its sharp chin. Pointing to where
everything happens at once. With nothing
left to squander, time hurries on ahead.
So our houses are never finished. And
after sunset we shrink from empty spaces.

Though these places are not without gravity
of course. Or fair geometries. Some have
laws, to their credit. And traces of ice.
But the stars, frankly, don't recognize
their own names. And in a dark corner
the infinite begins before you know it.

Recording Time

Time and again I looked for
the lost hours. The winding lines
at Motor Vehicle. Rolling numbers
at the casino. There were afternoons
when the lawns quickly unmowed
and a skylight burned out
(it was dark, though not for long).
At the corner an intersection
beeped me across. I was looking for
the white city on a hill.
From its eminence, a small port
mustered visitors in sunglasses
and flip flops.
Flounder was stacked like pelts
in the stalls. Someone whistled
"Clair de Lune," filling the air
with a long time. At a distance—
Middle-earth neighborhoods of story-
book houses. Thatched fairy-tale roofs
from a past far away. Everything
seemed right. The serpentine walls
snaking along shady lanes. Eternal
spring colored in. Even the clouds.
And a soldier at the bottom of the page
standing guard over the annual GNP
and looking at his watch.

Public Face of the Private

The mockingbird rehearses
its very few bars of *Finlandia*
from the gold-leafed gates.
This is about as good
as real estate ever gets.
Inside the great hall
a bed sleeps eight.
Coffered chests on onion feet.
Marbles from ruined
empires in little drawers.
Six from Rome in its grandeur.
Some from Babylon.
And even from America
once camped at the Tigris.
There is beauty in all of this.
Like slices of moon
served on black plates.
But first the potatoes
have to be peeled downstairs.
Tinkers and the fishmonger
with their tendentious invoices
will have begun knocking at
the service door for what is owed.
And an inspector will arrive to say
with a melancholy air
nothing here is up to code.

One Apple in a Still Life

Gravenstein eyes an apple:
the apple from apple
each apple from its stem.
Satisfaction, he believes
arises from affinities
though much dissatisfies him.
He is capable of hunger.
Rich enough for a vulgarity
he could spring for a Maybach.
Love is not beyond question.

But the apple is itself
and love seems not a probability.
Hunger is a subtext in any case.
Gravenstein sees
each apple is not to other apples
as the apple is to him.
Nor is an apple seen
all that an apple is.
And who knows what it wants to be
—if red, yellow, and/or green
or something other in between.

A Social History

The young bring their vigor
or whatever they bring—
chords on a guitar
the latest in DNA
contempt for the imperfect.
Yet somewhere they leave it.
They hardly know this
though they leave it here
where the mountains are worn
and rise slowly from the world
of stained old men
smelling of rancor and urine.

Bridal Shower

They brought cigars
for the groom. Some older guests
celluloid collars. Gas coupons
in case of war. Others a lettuce-
keeper in Tupperware.
Mix and match for the bride.
Bed linen in mauve sateen.
A couple that has everything
for top of the wedding cake. Herbs
for ratatouille.
A cutting-edge vibrator
that raised gasps.
Subscriptions to *Mother Jones*
and *Horse and Rider*.
A wind-up metal turkey with real
feathers and a plastic cornucopia.
Two ribbon candy rednecks. Tied in
bows and knots. Liniments and
three salves passed around to
ohs and ahs Then on to
pin-the-tail and charades.
Some thinking of the maid's day off.
A few, civilization and its discontents.

The Interior Decorator Advises

The decorator said, *you* need
something soft
like air.
Grass and stars
belong over there.
Hang the cost. Move the window.
Steeple and bell
constitute a view.
Extend the door.
By and by you will grow.
Embrace more.
Coarsen. Widen.
Cold and sand
will find their welcome
like it or not.
In the back room where you retreat
maybe a dog or cat.
Children seem beyond the scope
of what you meant.
And probably not a loveseat.

Over here—with your ghosts
just the right puce. But not
too much. It's necessary
to blend. Anything else
like ochre will require
more fabric.
Remember, whatever is left out
can't be seen.

Making of the Little There

Those pips and squeaks
behind the fence
are hens scratching for fare
invisible to the eye
but finding it there.

Elsewhere nature's paucity
in larger matters like
falling stars, the chill of space
still counts on prodigality
of a spare largess.

Three

Light at the Edges

in earth's contested bed
of light
one galaxy gathers
the heroic world
scuttering across night
and assigns roles—
Perseus, defender
of the old order
Pegasus grazing, alert for
a night's ride
Orion hunting through the sky
for the irretrievably lost
—epic efforts
useful as legends are
for sketching in
the now-obscure
as day recollects
those scissored silhouettes
of the once-familiar
like your school picture
now hardly recognizable
under the bare light's bulb
and where we remain necessary
if only for our shadows

Fourth Quarter

They went so far that year
they had to turn back as oak.
Going a little less—will yield ash
low in cost, useful for
frames, wheels
so favored by the gods—
there's nothing to rust.
In the kitchen where the timer
is set to run over
lights flicker and wink.
A jet stream plunging in from
the Pacific licks at a backyard
glacier. Enough of that
and fossils will soon see
whence they came.
Like the darkening wood
of Dante's suicide trees.
Once they decide to shade
the shades, all hell breaks loose.
Boles shrunken. Bark shriveled.
Forget sunglasses. An inch ahead
everything is darkness. You'll see.

A Man Whistling

He whistled like other male birds.
Like the constable. The salesmen
on sailor's leave. Those back from
dislocated lives. The lonely
trying to take the measure
of incalculable distance
where silence still is sound.

And he stayed tuned to ballads.
Carter Family lyrics, dance pops.
National anthems of the good republics.
Even those of the disgraced Hapsburgs.
The nervous tics of memory
now used as improvisations
never breaking into song.

Life on the Wing

To repeat endlessly
the only story you know
is not as limiting
as it seems

like everyone
with a story to tell
your life reveals
who you are

to those who want to know
and modesty
suggests the audience
will be alert but small

listening to the lines
that once were yours
with your walk-on part
and now are ours.

Furnished Apartment

I've just moved in, don't own much.
Accept on loan what others left.
The Dutch oven with cracked lid.
Four Ovaltine glasses.
I check the empty closet.
Look around to see
what needs moving.
Everything seems almost right.
A half-jug of wine on the table.
Some Wonder Bread, a Sunbeam toaster.
By the window a green stuffed chair.
There's plenty of light to see
what's true.
A window big enough
to let in the infinite
appeal of sky. The morning star.
Up close it's a trompe l'oeil.
The sashes painted shut.
Leaves hang back, as if in fear.
A world not worn enough to be real.
I won't unpack more than I have.
You're never certain how long
you're staying. When you go
you're sure to leave something
that wasn't yours.

Suddenness

Tongues have been sucked into the sky.
Neither theme park nor church destroyed.
Only a grade school (empty), barn, four cows.
The problem is not real estate.
Or Oklahoma, Alabama.
You could pick straw from weatherboards
three years after. Rounded domes
of storm cellars in backyards
dot old farmsteads. Stocked with things
that keep: kraut, canned tomatoes
a Montgomery Ward catalogue.
How long will this green darkness last?
children grow up asking.
Is it true the sky can blow you away?
But parents are always busy.

Distant Perspective

The wandering dead
looking for the doors back
into rooms they left
take side streets
the roads left off local maps
and face the dust
for months on end
anxious, their hands full
everyone clinging to burdens
purses, bags, valises
yet extend a hand to us
as if they were you and I
looking for familiar faces.
And we thought they
only wanted rest.

Slow Beginning of Ruin

It starts in several ways.
Somewhere a star sputters.
If stars can borrow our terms
like "the peach is losing its blush."
Entire towns will snore
through their RMS, missing
alarums of space. And grudges
night holds against us.
Those little details
of pending extinction show up
in your morning's mirror.
A pimple. Razor nicks.
Maybe an ice cap out of hearing
melting and Houston
now flooding. It's seldom
anything sudden.
Just when everything goes
depends on catch
of the day, doesn't it?
Knowing that the day
is prone to say
"this too can't last."

Mind Returning from an Obsession

The fiesta has gone on for so long.
Form in love with its material.
Dancing timbrels. Castanets
taunting time. The trees attached
to dull leaves. Music stressed, blaring
surly manifestoes from amplifiers.

And a summer lull in the war between
what appears and what seems.
A curtain goes up on
what started as vacation, an idyll
to idle in and full of fun, we thought.
Already the exorcist in the plaza
is asking from his perch
for the easy stuff first:

> *do you renounce the luxuries*
> *of this world?* (the better malbecs
> —apparently not the Rolls or Rolex)
>
> *fast consolations of sex?*
>
> *are you afraid of dying?*

With these premises
the questions properly begged
the cost of everything, as a judge
was overheard saying, has just gone up.
Weakened by the smoke of jazz
I want to say yes. Yes, yes.

Voices we hear in the barrios celebrate
summer according to the secular rites
of passion and possession. Others
take the narrow gauge for the glacier
before it melts. Protocol forbids
feeding rheas on the way to their boas.

But where else would you go?
Isn't that like asking—what is truth?
We want to come home
from our obsessions. I'm late for the chanted
mantras of my time. As in *the way forward*
is the way forward. But still
at the door I expect to be turned back.
The price of admission now escapes me.

With Due Diligence

What should be done?
Rescue the poor from us?
Themselves. Restore
wolves to Yellowstone?
A Fifth Crusade to retake
paradise? Jihad to
take it back.
Nostalgias in waiting
like forces of necessity.
Fire of old causes ember
in the reptilian mind
at the back of the brain.
Against a fast back-burn
the senses stall. Before
reaching just in time
what the world
no longer wants.

Items Mislaid

You lose your way back. Your virginity.
Maybe your religion. Lost and Found
seldom finds the things it should.
Or what you need.
                                        One day the key
to happiness turns up
missing. Like your address book. Or health.
And eventually the silver rings
of old enchantments go.
                                        Things seek
a place. They'll find you. Or you'll find them.
Peeking out from behind. Or right in front.
Though perhaps not in time.

The Republic Marks Down

You have to wonder what's up
for sale. Mannequins groping
in shop windows. Soft underwear
porn full of pushback desire.
Florida lots still under water.
Glock 19s discounted up to forty percent.
The price of everything
just reduced nearly to
tears. In jaunty, angled script
the red background
its dunning white letters
are sent to the usual deadbeats
with their closet dreams
and nothing to buy
but coffee and Krispy Kremes.
But you can push people just so far.
The road to the Coca-Cola
refinery is now barricaded.
Burnt-out Humvees on the shoulders.
Looted cigarettes, Hershey bars.
Yet the soft evenings are turned over
to katydids—
and always the American bargain.
The night and its wild perfection.

Trekking West: Part B

Back on the Garden State
you lost a dirt bike.
And Cincinnati was from nowhere
but safe at least
since nothing happens there
first.
Ragtime, swing, the blues, jazz
follow rivers like the weather.
Manifest destiny, they say, runs
east to west. Read your Hegel.
So in St. Louis
you catch something.
Burn and foam later
taking a piss in Kansas.
Trucked your U-Haul
up the Great Divide.
You boiled over
at Donner Pass.
American iron. Plastic hubcaps.
You headed on toward that blue
and white terminus of light
where the city of Oz
meets the golden eye of dust.
Fingers tapping out
Happy Trails.
A place for ducking out.
Packing it in. Jumping off.
Need we go farther.

Rapture at Breakfast

First, rumors of Armageddon.
In the east, thunder and fire. Shooting
stars. The Army of Canaan crossing
the Plains of Abraham. Canadian
winter close behind. Phalanxes
of the saved. Neighbors, people
you see every morning at the diner—
one minute leaning over
sausages, pancakes, three eggs
reading market pages, the weather.
Next, they're slipping off like heavy
rockets. Joining the 144,000 others
from all over for endtime.
Those left—looking for scalped tickets.
A guy in the booth by the window
is on his cellphone now. Hold on
to your seat. It could be a wild ride.

Reading between the Lines

What are these pains
the one along the spine
just below the kidney
on the right

bodily wear and tear
easy-to-underestimate
warnings—
so nothing lasts

those Potemkin fronts
certainly fooled us at twenty
death such an extravagance
better spectacle than fact

looking at the fine print
you'll find the shelf life
woven into the DNA
now chiseled in low relief.

Letter to a Friend

You think nature is simple in its urges.
I believe nature complicates as it develops.
Except for emphasis, a necessary antithesis
—there need be little contention between us.

You prefer Picasso, I like Matisse.
You like Bob Dylan, Leonard Cohen here.
You read Toynbee, Spengler for me.
I like 3.2. You—something full, a nose of
berries, the touch of chocolate.

It seems—dear Archilochus—that
the point between us, the polarities
that irritate, can be resolved
with sensitive finesse
into a single urgent issue.

I'm looking for a kingdom that
ruffles its borders. You're after the phylum
that always defines. We imagine
such matters still matter.

General Disquiet

A feeling you have—
stepping away from
a *primi piatti* with sour
compliments to the chef
though you can't remember
what you had
or like a child
his paddle and ball
with no one to disturb
and who will notice
the complaint—
is it something about the world
and by the way
you notice
space is much too large
for one person
and yet—
there is something else
something here
isn't quite right.

Racing toward Conclusions

They always looked both ways for
the bad news.
Knowing the river road ran to
the sea road, and sea road
to where they couldn't see
what lay ahead.
There was a flurry of fear at the curtains.
Hands smoothing the sawtooth rim
of a cut-glass bowl.
Two fingers brushing a white rose.
Broken petals falling into night
bright with a storm lashing green.
Drinks for two over paleo memories
were shared with a crash.
It was only truth insisting on its verities.
How dark it became
a single light racing ahead like a lantern
held above exhausted night.
Upstairs the master of extremes
was executing all the domiciled ghosts
of next to no use.

Alexander in Afghanistan

There were rumored anthropophagi.
Warrior women in purple turbans.
Zouaves like Zebra men
and the painted Celts
from Ecbatana westward.
It was still a strange world.
News came by camel.
And you were the news.
Hephaestion gone
there was no hand
to touch the sleeping thigh.
No lips like satin to skin.
History almost done
the tables cleared
slides of *déjà vu* now flashed by.
The torsos without legs
you see along the Silk Road.
Bell tinkle of blinded beggars
outside temple gates.
Rust buckets from an earlier time
in armor and bronze
buried in the moving sand.
Then Bucephalus dead.

And soon you, at Babylon
homeward bound
and perhaps just in time.
Who knows what heartbreak
—the past never tells
since the world
still wants to be rediscovered.

Evening Fell with the City

The darkened city surrendered
to ruin. Monumental travertine
arches stripped to brick. Hospitals
boarded up. Paneless windows
of the LGBT Center no longer
reflecting changed milieus.
Trolleys curving past
an embarcadero
snaked lines of emigrants
to tooting ships.
Back from the politics
of old resentments and public rot
the President-for-Life
bolted his door, prepared for bed.
But first checked to see
that all the lights had been put out.

Five

In over Your Head

I'm sitting in the terminal, tarot cards
on the bench. My thirteenth card turned
up—then two blasts
on the horn.
                    Our bus was leaving soon.
An express for some abyss. The road
was high and dry. As of yet not a cloud
in the sky.
                Snarky waves smartly
waving back. Sand and water
high fiving. True blue. If only they
would come clean.
                        How easy to
get out of touch. Swimming too far out
for gulls. Life guards playing
Parcheesi. Whistles fainter.
                                I was
at the Jersey shore. What else
could summer do with summer?
Where else would dread of going
go? Where would a swimmer?

Jeremiad against Travel

Those favored back roads
driving Vermont
to watch trees
turning their leaves
or reaching the bald cranial front
of Half Dome in Yosemite
lobotomized out of public view
still seem excessive
since in our dreams
we never have to leave for night
running in place as we do
touring the dark
closets there
even when the ending
is announced time after time
because who can be sure
apart from certain linear equations
if travel wherever
is the only option
if going is even worthwhile.

ONCE WE THOUGHT OF IT

we thought better of it later.
Smashed shop fronts. Mattresses
on tops of cars. The looting
had begun.
                    The prime time of the world
hid its discontents, of course. California
water. MTV. Dirty dot.coms. Old ladies
pinching roaches.
                              In broad daylight
sometimes the worst. Its vast pop
sewer culture. Afternoon talk shows for
the full-time bored. A life with crunched
Doritos in the sofa tufts.
                                        At Cancun
we dead-ended, rocking in the shade.
Volume amped past frivolous, scorching.
Hundreds of miles away Chiapas guns
heard the morning report their rattle.

Past Time

Once out of the sea
your future's here.
Altoona, Corbin, Wichita Falls.
Screwing in a bulb.
Sundays mowing grass.
There's nothing you can do
about it. It's like choosing
sides in an argument.
What comes next
falls into place.
What comes after
comes predictably after.
If there are windows
like the Sicilian Defense
or chances like Saturday Night
Powerball or Pick 3—
watch out for daily taunts
of fate. The grave aspects
of sepulchers, the ubiquitous
tombs line up like odds.

Questions to an Answer

The tease of afternoons winding
out of summer and taking us
to evening and blank looks

—is that the face of God
stoic, staring out across the darkness
of the infinite

or a clockface God
imposed on a void
with mechanical exactitude

or the brighter face
of a long-running feature
projecting awe

—you put your glasses on
to pull up old news from the annals
looking for a satisfactory answer

and wonder—won't all of this
be sorted out as time
in a new, strange light?

Lost or Misplaced

It was last seen, if seen it was
in an ancestral attic
with the onyx
from a meteorite
and flies
in Prussian amber
and now believed to have been put
with family pictures from Alexandria
and daguerreotypes of fat ladies
with parasols at Marienbad
and their pet walrus
from the Black Sea
and Aunt Edna on a camel
all surely grown restless
after years of wander
won't they seem to be asking
if not everyone at once
where is the key
to contentment
if not happiness itself
and where could you have put it?

Advisory to Myself

You can see the past
is careless about time.
Take dragons and their kin
the dinosaurs
from children.
Trilobites from the ocean
and what do you have?
Of course the past is over
but lasts forever.
Antics of the deviant temporal
like those of the miraculous
contest natural order.
Make people nervous.
Keep the dead on edge
asking *then why am I dead?*

Special Agents

They hang around. They do.
Funeral parlors. Pedestrian
crossings. Back pews
at minor shrines.
Connecting with crooked ways
of the infinite.

She smiles, swinging her thin
black purse. I've known her
since I was six. What she thinks
of that, she plays close. Very
close.

Her black hat, banded with
inviolate daisies tinted
blue in summer. For winter
a grape-leaved legend
fringed about.

She always asks after my ex-.
I say not well. Not well at all.
She's sorry to hear it. Of course
she is, fingering her hat.
I thank her anyway.
Talk louder, she says.

In the Spirit of Ludwig Richter

He was a stalwart of intent
on the lookout for justice
in the world as it is.
His collections of corkscrews
crossbows, Swiss Army knives
took our breath.
Last night the ocean poured out
its design in a rage. Lightning
to torch a progress or two.
I was surprised by the storm's
fluency and expertise. But weren't
we looking for those very things?
The night clerk with his flagon
of spiced tea
perilously wandering our halls
intended a mercy.
(Might not a mere spark
of love end the world?)
We thought the nighttime ruckus
was only Ludwig Richter
opening his cabinet of curiosities.
But he was merely looking for
what is right and true
and long, long overdue.

Planned Obsolescence

We wear out, wear out: I with
the heart, you with a hip.
Taking nitro, use of a prosthesis
do only so much.
Berryman's eyes
behind glass, starlight against
the moon. Fingers read obsolete
in time's brassy Braille.
It's worse
inside. Old cells forget, toss away
keys. Names at risk—day, address
and breakfast in doubt.
You can see
it's part of a plan. Though GM
takes the rap, while necessity keeps
two fingers in the design.
With
predatory gravity, its candy and pop
enticing a star—the moon and other
onlookers like us remain
beyond repair.

Patience

Blood pressure of an old Zen master.
Waist of a swimmer.
Night after night
sleep of the pure heart.
No dreams of ice and razor wire.
Children excel in school, deliver
papers every morning at five.
Take ballroom dancing.
A mate who never reads the ads
suburbia writes. Bills paid up.
Credit unblemished.
Mortgage paid off. Neighbors
who mow your grass when you go
off to Silver Bay. You count
your blessings.
Patience, she said. It will last
only a little longer.

Six

Reflection on a Window

Yes, the sea looks like glass.
Those clouds far off
don't lie. Red is the color
of things that hurt.

The sun slips behind mountains
in time to snap fingers
over an empty house.
Its windows like eyes put out.

I returned just once. The door
on its back, wind sweeping
toward me like an old woman—
teeth in her pocket, all arms.

A mute bird on a fence post, one foot
on the wire, stared toward the glass.
As if it knew the room
where the song was lost.

In Search of Restoration

The woods have resisted most
of time's improvement.
For years the streams fled
our poisons, calling out from their beds.
Animals
thought to sense earthquakes
sought low shelter.
At the approach of tornadoes
birds flew to their coups
in the grey-green light.
After a storm the feathers plucked
from guineas two counties over
were found like darts
in the house's weatherboards.
Until then the restless squirrels
seldom forgot their maps
and could afford to lie back and wait.
And last year's corn, already laid by
in the fields, had time to mutate.

Prospect of Infinity

Like the sun in decline
you survey the firmament—
light striking first this
then that moon:
a chin strap
holds your attention: arms belted
to your sides, muscles muscle off
into spasms:
you try counting—
stop at the prospect of infinity
try to order the planets
what comes between Saturn and
Pluto?
the universe shifts
categorically, an MRI humming
into your space music of logarithms:
a noise to clarify disorders.
Space, sufficient, never reconsiders.

Dissonances of Early Morning

Wings against the wind.
Like the crack, whir of whips.
Morning tossing back
its head. A muezzin starting
to chant in the earliest hours.

The same wind has leveled
the wheat. Then as breath
sent flutes to quiver.
Nature knows better
than to offer a choice.

We're back from the disordered
fields. The children have not
finished torturing their dog.
Perils linger in an unconsoled
world. In the dying fire
ashes have already felt the heat.

Perspective of a Late Roman

Always the pull of affection.
The years of pilgrimage.
I have upheld the old gods.
There were petty sneers
of the scoffers.
Scorn of those
worshipping the new.
Now the candles
have gone out.
The naves fallen in.
So I see the dead
will bury the dead.
And that time
takes its own medicine.
But who, who will pray for rain.

Some Peace and Quiet

Listen to the jungle aubade
the hoya tendrils in love, snapping
the air—on dusk's near horizon of din
macaws and howlers at prayer
                                                                        the
cellphones, leaf blowers, saws
and heartbreak of the 11 o'clock news
always the slow suck of evil
                                                                   there
is no absence of sound anywhere
even in the far beyond where space
chatters endlessly on
                                                    and
now everyone is talking at once
as if voices could drown out new pain
with memories of the old—
                                                                    since
silence is not a natural state
but only quiet of a graveyard staying put
on Saturdays and Sundays
when the mowers aren't out.

Return from Surprise

Eucalyptus trash
windblow of another time
scattered papers
rake the street
with questions.
Old photo magazines
lie bundled up, shivering
at the curb. From one
a ghost in Levi's
standing before you
wears a skeleton
like yours and asks
what went wrong.
The ivory clack
a mumbled voice coming after
the thought
that has waited too long
for thinking.
And now is overtaken
by events.

Design of Winter

Ice lying along the limbs deflects the sun.
Hidden rhombuses of early January
swap places with tree birds singing.
There will be further violence.

Work of the weather-stricken city spins out
on local salt. Others flee south
for passion, to play in perennial
pastels. Well, a little.

For workers attending their jobs
in freezing slush this morning—like the cold
of a merciless idea, what meaning
can ice have?

Hillsides recoil for miles with querulous
sounds. Scrape of cold. The dull knife of
routine. Icy light striking blind.
This is how it's done so no one sees.

Waiting on Time

Like a cautious traveler—I tip
the god of pain.
An old man, hurting
for years, hugs me.
A cathedral, five centuries
on the corner, ruined, emptied
to pigeons.
Waiting for return of the holy
like the three sacred volcanoes
wreathed in afternoon clouds.
Two of them extinct.
Boys
sulky in the park
shine shoes.
Some, *bandidos*
steal from *gringos*.
The *alcaldía*, colonial seat
of misrule
has been closed for repairs
for two hundred years.
In the public market maze
old women lost inside their lives
shop alone
for maize and beans, follow streets
that never leave town.

Whoever you are, I have always depended on the kindness of strangers.

Blanche DuBois, *A Streetcar Named Desire*

Acknowledgments

Boulevard
Patience

Borderlands
The Sixth Proof of God
Jeremiad against Travel (published as "Public Summit")
Reflection on a Window

5AM
Some Peace and Quiet (published as "Bulletin")

Pleiades
Public Face of the Private

Southern Humanities Review
Letter to a Friend

New Republic
Travelers

Spoon River Poetry Review
A Man Whistling (published as "Learning to Whistle")
The Interior Decorator Advises

I wish to thank the readers and editors for their openness to my work.

About the Author

Robert Bense lives in Sacramento, California, and Waterloo, Illinois.

Garamond Premier Pro font 12/13 used in text

Made in the USA
Coppell, TX
08 August 2022